Beyond These Pages

-Poetry by Ashton Rhodes

This is for you

Wanderers
organic minds
the dreamers that bring the
paradigm shifts.

For so many now it's uniformity,
conformity,
superiority.

Awaken to the world again.
The landscape's just for you.
Your feet miss the dirt of the Earth.
Stop and stare at the stars in
wonderment,
at the fathomless night in its
awestruck
splendidness.
Listen to the train in the distance.
Feel the breath in your lungs.

Nightingales that reach out to you,
begging you to join the serenade.
Leap out of your confines
and drink the black liquor of night in
one drought.
Fill your soul again
with the sense of insignificance.
That you are small and meek,
the world is wide
but it is yours,
run to it.

Listen.

The nighttime composes symphonies
from unexpected instruments;
clocks ticking,
thunder,
heartbeats.

This darkness,
home to stars and winds that haunt
trees,
let this elusive beauty be your unrest.

Stay awake,
watch the dance between sun and
moon,
feel time spinning
but be the axis.

Move and your voice will follow.
Run and your heart will awaken.
Speak wildly about what excites you.
Shake up the room and watch them
squirm.
Passion is not dead,
it's buried under your deadlines,
your schedules,
your belongings.

Unearth it.

The eye has been trained into tunnel
vision
peering downward at tiny
illuminated screens
that fill the black rooms of isolation.
The mind absorbing
while the body dies.
Stillness contemplating a moving life
anchored to the seat of technology.

Convenience; the thief of time
has given you moments
that are wasted trying to run.

Stop.

Look up,
look up from your glowing screens
computer,
television,
tablet, or phone.
Look up into the big great beautiful
world
in front of you.
Live the life that you dream.

Don't form the mind
to fit the molds
imposed by gods or government.
Reach beyond the now,
let the mind expand
and breathe into greater fields
where consciousness runs free.

Pay attention.

Listen to birds sitting on wires
applauding the morning.
Watch the pure rain wash over the
lonely fields
until all that's left is mud and
memories.
The distant roll of thunder playing
timpani
in the earth's symphony of storm.
It's all a dance.
Blades of grass auditioning for the
ballet of wind.
Watch the trees nod in silent
approval.

In your veins you feel it.

The fire is speaking to you.
The fire of stars,
of your own heart.
The flame of an idea.
You hear it
but you ignore it.
You medicate it.
You suffocate it with self-imposed
structure.

Read.

Absorb the pages unfolding,
unfurling words into being,
shattering thoughts like glass.
Shatter them.
Pick them up and rearrange them
into something that is your own.
Burn with them,
emerge drenched in the ash of total
consumption.

Move.

Get caught up in the excitement of
tomorrow,
the unknown,
the ways of the lives around you.
Pass through like a ghost,
imprint yourself forever on the
hearts of those
who wish they could follow;
to them be a God of the Earth
traveling
to collect your haphazard life in
fragments
stirred up in the dust you leave
behind.

Be unapologetic for your raw and
dirty,
exposed soul that spooks the walking
shells
you encounter.
Be the most real thing
like a dog unashamed of his wagging
tail
and slobbering smile.
Soak up life the way we're all meant
to
if only we could stop checking
ourselves
in the mirror.

Look within.

The spaces between our real lives
and our sexual self are so far between
leaving a gap,
a distance that grows incrementally
with every wedge
forced through external oppressors.

Live your sexual self,
the core of you that is desirous of
everything,
in every aspect of your life.

Have passion.

Look at what you love with lustful
eyes
and a heart that always yearns for
the unknown.
Question the reality that you have
grown into
and all the heavy supposed truths
that seem so concrete in their time
that will pass by into realms
forgotten.

Forget the artificial bearings you
root yourself to.
Root yourself to your own feet
and move them
in accordance to your soul.

Go wandering amongst the lost ones,
the ones who anchored themselves
to the perishable.
If you can bring them out of their
prison
with words,
with music,
with something that touches them to
their core,
their base sexual self,
you will have connected to the
human spirit.

We are all transient,
accepting that,
truly embracing it
will bring you to the passion of life
and the desire to always be
searching.

Which thoughts are your own
and which have been planted in
your mind?

Can you tell the difference?

We are spoon-fed our passions
through a needle forged by revenue.
We should devour art
starved as we are
for true inspiration.
All copies of copies
these so called best sellers,
shatter their equation,
live outside the ratings.

Don't let yourself be owned by
Dogma.
Create your own path.

Religion is a brand
processed,
marketed,
cloned,
and sold.
A stamp of intolerance seared into
your skin,
the constant smell of burning flesh
scorching your thoughts.

Nature is a balm.
Sink your palms into the earth
and the roots of the thirsty trees
will drink from you the shame you
feel
upon your awakening.

Lie back in the rushing stream,
let your blood renew itself
with the blood of all life.

Stare at the night sky and sense
the tugging of the thin string that
anchors you
to the stars
and the gravitational pull of the
moon.
You are an axis all your own
yet entangled in this infinite web.

Do not stand indifferent to the world,
you are of it
and of all the living energy you
share
with those who pulse with that same
rhythm;
a part of everything that is
not merely a silver piece to be
collected at tithing,
used to feed the machine
that destroys
this perfect dance.

Look for signs.

The clouds that shuffle by,
the beams of light that glint off your
windshield,
they are harbingers of life
telling you every minute that this is
your time.
The crescent moon,
the skeleton trees
all messengers delivering a sermon;
Awaken.

You are not controlled.
You are not too late.
You are not lost except unto your
purpose.
Your purpose here is not as you are
told it to be.

You are not here to pay off your debt
or to be obedient to others.
You are not breathing so that you
can consume
the unnecessary.
You do not exist so that you can
collect wealth.

You do not own others
and they do not own you.
Do not stare out the window
dreaming that one day
you will live.
Do not save all your years so that
someday
you can do what you have always
wanted.

Look beyond all of the accumulation
you have gathered
into the stillness beyond.
The place your mind takes you
when the foreground disappears.
This is your true self.

Walk towards it.

Forever is a promise made of glass
and you are not allowed to hold it
nor is anyone
and if they claim to be in possession
of it
know that they are mistaken.

None of us own time
and time is only your enemy
if you wait for it to be right.
Time has no agenda
because it knows not of itself
and therefore you cannot blame it
for your failure to act.

Beyond these pages
your world is waiting for you.

Run.

www.ingramcontent.com/pod-product-compliance
Lightning Source LLC
Chambersburg PA
CBHW020443030426
42337CB00014B/1368